CHRISTMAS
GIF'

To Joyce & Sam —
May you be blessed with
many many Christmas Gif's every
day!
with love,
Gwen

CHRISTMAS GIF'

AN ANTHOLOGY OF CHRISTMAS POEMS, SONGS, AND STORIES

WRITTEN BY AND ABOUT
AFRICAN-AMERICANS

Compiled by
Charlemae Hill Rollins
Illustrated by Ashley Bryan

With a New Introduction by
Dr. Augusta Baker

Morrow Junior Books
NEW YORK

1 2 3 4 5 6 7 8 9 10

Library of Congress Cataloging-in-Publication Data
Christmas gif' : an anthology of Christmas poems, songs, and stories
written by and about African-Americans / compiled by Charlemae Rollins ;
illustrations by Ashley Bryan ; a new introduction by Dr. Augusta
Baker.
p.   cm.
Includes index.
Summary: A collection of Christmas poems, songs, and stories
relating to African-Americans. Includes holiday recipes.
ISBN 0-688-11667-1 (trade).   ISBN 0-688-11668-X (library).
1. Christmas—Literary collections. 2. American literature—Afro-
American authors. 3. Afro-Americans—Literary collections.
[1. Christmas—Literary collections. 2. Afro-Americans—Literary
collections.]   I. Rollins, Charlemae Hill.   II. Bryan, Ashley, ill.
III. Title: Christmas gift.
PZ5.C4735 1993
810.8'033—dc20   92-18976   CIP   AC

A Note to Readers

When my mother gathered together these stories, songs, poems, and recipes in 1963, the term "African-American" to designate American people of African descent had not come into popular use. In the United States, African-Americans have always questioned their identity and as early as 1827 were wondering, "What should we call ourselves?" Since then, many words and phrases have been created in a continuing attempt to answer this question. Throughout this collection the reader will find such words as "Colored" and "Negro," which, in the early 1960s, were acceptable and widely used terms. While some of the language and dialects may seem outdated, to make any changes would certainly alter the artistic intent of the authors, poets, and lyricists. It is most important to preserve the authenticity and the historical and literary integrity of these works. Their language does not obscure the messages of peace, unity, and goodwill that still ring true thirty years after the first publication of *Christmas Gif'*. I hope that this collection will still touch the hearts of all families as they celebrate the joy of Christmas.

—JOSEPH W. ROLLINS

A race is like a man.
Until it uses its own talents,
takes pride in its own history,
and loves its own memories it
can never fulfill itself completely.

JOHN W. VANDERCOOK

The institution of "Christmas gift" survived the 1870's and lived on into the recent past, into the 1920's and 1930's and even, in some cases, beyond. Even after it had died away in the towns, it continued in the country areas; on farms or remnants of plantations, the whites were still waked by the cry and the smiling demand. As late as the mid-1940's, when I spent Christmas at a friend's plantation, I emerged from my room to the accompaniment of four or five simultaneous shouts of "Chris'mus gift!" But on my return, less than ten years later, only one attendant, the elderly cook who was the last of the former helpers, called it in a muted voice and somewhat shamefacedly. Three other house servants, newly arrived from town, appeared hesitant to echo the words.

Finally I broke the ice. "Don't you want a Christmas present?" With smiles that spread from one to the other, they fell in with the spirit as we recalled the old custom. But when I go back the next time I feel certain that this tradition will be gone completely.

HARNETT T. KANE

For the Christmas feasting and revelry were only one phase of the slaves' Christmas; the other was the devout, plain faith of the people. As John Esten Cooke saw it, Christmas was to them "what it was in the pious Middle Ages—a solemn mystery as well as a joyful reality. With the rejoicing of the season is inseparately connected in his mind what this rejoicing arises from."

HARNETT T. KANE

Contents

Foreword

THE NAME OF this anthology represents much to me—the pleasure of giving and recollections of a happy tradition that had its origins in the days of slavery. The custom of "Christmas Gif' " has been a part of the holiday celebration in my family for as long as I can remember.

As a child I spent much time with my grandmother, who had been a slave. From her I learned that "Christmas Gif' " was a surprise game played by the slaves on Christmas Day. Two people, meeting for the first time that day, would compete to be the first to call out "Christmas Gif'!" The loser happily paid a forfeit of a simple present—maybe a Christmas tea cake or a handful of nuts. Truly, there was more pleasure in being "caught" and having to give a present—the giving, though comically protested, was heartwarming to a people who had so little they could with dignity share with others.

The practice of "Christmas Gif' " spread from the slave cabins to the "Big House" and soon became a traditional part of the celebration of Christmas, a joyful time felt and shared even by an enslaved people.

Over the years, in my experience as a librarian, I have been asked by teachers and parents and children for Christmas stories and poems specifically related to Negroes. I have found such material in old magazines, in collections of the works of Negro writers, but never have I found one single book about the Negro and Christmas. I felt there was a place for such a book, and that is how *Christmas Gif'* began. It is a book for people of all ages, for families to read together, for everyone to enjoy.

This book could not have been compiled without the help of countless friends, librarians, teachers, parents, and above all, children. The children's eager quest for knowledge inspired and stimulated all of us.

Special thanks also is given to my friend Mrs. Carrié Ray of New Orleans, Louisiana, for her help in checking the accuracy of the recipes; to Dr. Dexter Reynolds, for his phenomenal recall of traditional eastern shore cooking; to Miss Mary Whitfield, who so generously shared with me her Kentucky cooking lore. I am indebted also to my friend Langston Hughes for his encouragement, inspiration, and generous help.

It is my earnest hope that this book may help every reader to appreciate the Negro's contribution to the love and reverence, the joy and brotherhood, that is the universal spirit of Christmas.

CHARLEMAE HILL ROLLINS
1963

Acknowledgments

The Editor and Publisher are grateful to the following copyright holders for permission to include copyright material in this anthology. Every effort has been made to trace the holders of copyright in all selections; if, however, any query should arise, it should be addressed to the Publisher.

"The Legend of the Black Madonna" is adapted from *Merry Go Round a Pilgrim's Progress Around the World* by Margaret T. Applegarth. Copyright 1925, renewed 1952, by Judson Press. Used by permission of Judson Press.

"How Come Christmas" is from *How Come Christmas* by Roark Bradford. Copyright 1930 by Harper & Row, Publishers, Inc.

"Otto" is from *Bronzeville Boys and Girls* by Gwendolyn Brooks. Copyright 1956 by Gwendolyn Brooks Blakeley. Reprinted by permission of HarperCollins Publishers.

"Under the Mistletoe" is from *Copper Sun* by Countee Cullen. Copyright 1927 by Harper & Brothers; copyright renewed 1955 by Ida M. Cullen. Reprinted by permission of GRM Associates, Inc., agents for the Estate of Ida M. Cullen.

"Goat Comes to the Christmas Party" is from *Araminta's Goat* by Eva Knox Evans. Copyright 1938 by Eva Knox Evans. Reprinted by permission of Eva Knox Witte.

"Every Man Heart Lay Down" is from *How God Fix Jonah* by Lorenz Graham. Copyright 1946 by Lorenz Graham. Reprinted by permission of Ruth M. Graham.

"Kid Stuff" by Frank Horne appeared originally in *The Poetry of the Negro*, edited by Langston Hughes and Arna Bontemps. Copyright 1949 by Langston Hughes and Arna Bontemps.

"An Anonymous Verse" and "The Christmas Story" by Langston Hughes. Copyright 1963 by Langston Hughes. "On a Christmas Night," "On a Pallet of Straw," "Shep-

Introduction

WHEN I WAS a young girl, my grandmother—like Charlemae Rollins's—used to tell me stories about Christmas in the "olden days." The celebration of Christmas then, as now, was a time of joy, giving, friendship, and reverence. From my grandmother's stories and my own reading of African-American literature, I knew that an understanding of the black experience was something I could share, and I'm sure this influenced my becoming a children's librarian in 1934. At the 135th Street branch of the New York Public Library, I met many black children who did not know much about their heritage. I began to introduce the children to such African-American writers as Lorenz Graham, Langston Hughes, Countee Cullen, Zora Neale Hurston, and Gwendolyn Brooks, as well as white writers, such as Eva Knox Evans and Julia Peterkin, who wrote with warmth and affectionate respect.

I first met Charlemae Hill Rollins through the American Library Association, in which we were both very active. We had another mutual interest: working with children and educating them about black writers and the black experience. Charlemae was a wonderful storyteller and promoted and supported all sorts of library programs for children. She took me under her wing, and I saw her as my mentor. I availed myself of every opportunity to discuss program ideas with her.

Charlemae was a most generous and selfless person, never thinking about her own advancement in librarianship. She was a fierce advocate for literary quality and minority representation in children's books. Publishers all viewed Charlemae with the highest esteem and would seek out her advice. Together, Charlemae in Chicago and I in New York, we worked closely with publishers who were just beginning to be interested in books by and about blacks.

Charlemae's involvement in black literary circles was evident to all of us working with her, and she influenced many writers, regardless of their race. Langston Hughes was one of those writers and he adored Charlemae. As his reputation grew and he became well known, Charlemae and her work with children's books also gained importance.

To help give black children a sense of their own culture, both Charlemae and I looked for material about African-American Christmas traditions, from slavery through the present, and we found stories in books and magazines for adults as well as for young people. But we discovered that there was no one definitive source on the subject. It was from our work, and a desire to pass along the literature of black writers to children, that the idea for Charlemae's influential anthology *Christmas Gif'* was born.

Some of my favorites in this collection are Lorenz Graham's "Every Man Heart Lay Down" and two poems I particularly like to share with children, Countee Cullen's "Under the Mistletoe" and Gwendolyn Brooks's "Otto." Langston Hughes was quite conscious of the relationship between the black experience and holiday time. Charlemae prevailed upon him to let her include some of his previously unpublished poems in her collection. I have shared his "Carol of the Brown King" over and over, and it has special appeal to me.

This reissue of *Christmas Gif'* is a cause for celebration. Librarians, teachers, parents—all those working and living with children and young adults—will look forward to using and sharing this unique book once again.

—AUGUSTA BAKER

CHRISTMAS
GIF'

Nativity

Within a native hut, ere stirred the dawn,
Unto the Pure One was an Infant born
Wrapped in blue lappah[1] that His mother dyed.
Laid on His father's home-tanned deerskin hide
The Babe still slept by all things glorified.
Spirits of black bards burst their bonds and sang
"Peace upon earth" until the heavens rang.
All the black babies who from earth had fled
Peeped through the clouds, then gathered round His head.

---

1. A straight woven cloth tied around the waist to form a skirt.

Telling of things a baby needs to do
When first he opens his eyes on wonders new;
Telling Him that to sleep was sweeter rest,
All comfort came from His black mother's breast.
Their gifts were of Love caught from the springing sod,
Whilst tears and laughter were the gifts of God.
Then all the wise men of the past stood forth
Filling the air East, West, and South and North;
And told Him of the joys that wisdom brings
To mortals in their earthly wanderings.
The children of the past shook down each bough,
Wreathed frangipani² blossoms for His brow;
They put pink lilies in His mother's hand,
And heaped for both the first fruits of the land.
His father cut some palm fronds that the air
Be coaxed to zephyrs while He rested there.
Birds trilled their hallelujahs; and the dew
Trembled with laughter till the Babe laughed too.
All the black women brought their love so wise,
And kissed their motherhood into His mother's eyes.

Aquah Laluah
(Gladys May Casely Hayford)

EDITOR'S NOTE: The author is a member of the Fanti tribe of Ghana, West Africa.
2. An African flower.

Memories of Christmas

My FIRST MEMORIES of Christmas center in Kansas, which is the very center of our U.S.A. Christmas trees, candles, cotton snow, and potbellied stoves are all mixed up in these early memories. The stove is there because my first Christmas tree always stood in the corner behind the potbellied stove. On account of the cotton snow, we had to be careful of the stove and of the candles on the tree. If the stove got red-hot, or the candles fell down, the cotton snow might catch on fire. The idea of snow catching on fire intrigues me to this very day. Early in life I had a love of excitement, and I always rather hoped the snow would catch on fire, but it never did.

4

For poor children, Santa Claus seldom lives up to expectation. I never remember finding on Christmas morning *all* of the things I had asked Santa Claus to bring. But always I would find at least one of the hoped-for gifts, and the surprise and happiness of that one would make up for those lacking. The big presents would always be under the tree. But hope for the missing BB gun or the long desired cowboy suit would not be downed until the very toe of each hanging stocking was also searched. But out of the stockings would usually come mostly oranges, nuts, and hard candies. Certainly, not even Santa Claus could get an air rifle into a stocking!

Christmas without presents must be a strange Christmas indeed for an American child. But as I grew older, I learned that there are children (even in this richest of all countries) whose parents and whose Santa Claus sometimes cannot afford presents. I was twenty-one before I knew a Christmas without presents. That year I was working in the merchant marine, and in early December we sailed out of New York harbor for Rotterdam. The boat had a new crew. Of the forty seamen aboard, none of us had ever met or worked together before. Christmas Eve we were at anchor in a strange Dutch port whose dock fronts and gabled houses were covered with the same white snow I had known in Kansas. Rotterdam's canal lights gleamed with a frosty glow as a half dozen of us took a motor launch across the harbor to the main part of the city where we found a cozy bar. There we greeted the Christmas dawn in a warm glow of Holland gin. Back aboard ship the next day, we had chicken for Christmas dinner, but no tree, and none of the crew exchanged presents.

That was my only Christmas without giving or receiving something. Even in the Soviet Union, where I spent a Yuletide away down in the heart of Uzbekistan in Central Asia, there were presents. Some thirty or forty miles from Tashkent there was at that time a colony of American

Negro cotton chemists and growers teaching the Asiatics how to raise cotton Alabama style. Among them was the late Colonel Young's son, and some others who had been teachers at Hampton and other of our Southern colleges. With their wives, they invited Bernard Powers, a Negro road engineer working in Tashkent, and myself to spend the holidays with them.

And it was just like being back home in Kansas although we were in the ancient land of Tamerlane and Genghis Khan and the Thousand and One Nights.

Other memorable Christmases for me in foreign lands have been the Yuletides of Mexico and of France. Paris has its charming features all the year round, but Christmas there—if you live with and know French people—has a heartwarming delight all its own.

In Mexico the holidays possess picturesque joys I have seen nowhere else. For nine days before Christmas there is a series of neighborhood parties each night from house to house known as *"las posadas."* At the *"posadas"* each guest takes a candle and a procession is formed that goes from room to room and door to door around the patio of the house singing:

> *Humildes peregrinos.*
> *María, Jesús, José . . .*

as Mary, with child, and her husband, Joseph, walked centuries ago seeking shelter in Bethlehem so that the Child might be born. But no door opens, so the procession moves on. The old story of man's lack of interest in his brother is acted out each night.

But each night it all ends in happiness and feasting, dancing and a party—and after nine such nights comes Christmas! Perhaps it simply means—this symbolic *"posada"*—that after the hard days, the long months (maybe even the bitter years), there comes somehow to everyone the clean white snow, the sparkling tree, the gifts, and the new birth of friendship and life that is Christmas, holiday of the newborn Child.

Langston Hughes

How Come Christmas

YOU SEE, ONE time hit was a little baby bawned name' de Poor Little Jesus, but didn't nobody know dat was his name yit. Dey knew he was a powerful smart and powerful purty little baby, but dey didn't know his name was de Poor Little Jesus. So, 'cause he was so smart and so purty, ev'ybody thought he was gonter grow up and be de kaing. So quick as dat news got spread around, ev'ybody jest about bust to git on de good side er de baby, 'cause dey figure efn dey start soon enough he'd grow up likin' 'em and not chop dey haids off.

So old Moses went over and give him a hund'ed dollars in gold. And old Methuselah went over and give him a diamond ring. And old Peter give him a fine white silk robe. And ev'ybody was runnin' in wid fine presents so de Poor Little Jesus wouldn't grow up and chop de haids off.

Ev'ybody but old Sandy Claus. Old Sandy Claus was kind er old and didn't git around much, and he didn't hyar de news dat de Poor Little Jesus was gonter grow up and be da kaing. So him and de old lady was settin' back by de fire one night, toastin' dey shins and tawkin' about dis and dat, when old Miz Sandy Claus up and remark, she say, "Sandy, I hyars Miss Mary got a brand new baby over at her house."

"Is dat a fack?" says Sandy Claus. "Well, well, hit's a mighty cold night to do anything like dat, ain't hit? But on de yuther hand, he'll be a heap er pleasure and fun for her next summer I reckon."

So de tawk went on, and finally old Sandy Claus remark dat hit was powerful lonesome around de house since all er de chilluns growed up and married off.

"Dey all married well," say Miz Sandy Claus, "and so I say, 'Good ruddance.' You ain't never had to git up and cyore dey colic and mend dey clothes, so you gittin' lonesome. Me, I love 'em all, but I'm glad dey's married and doin' well."

So de tawk run on like dat for a while, and den old Sandy Claus got up and got his hat. "I b'lieve," he say, "I'll drap over and see how dat baby's gittin' along. I ain't seed no chillun in so long I'm pyore hongry to lean my eyes up agin a baby."

"You ain't goin' out on a night like dis, is you?" say Miz Sandy Claus.

"Sho I'm goin' out on a night like dis," say Sandy Claus. "I'm pyore cravin' to see some chilluns."

"But hit's snowin' and goin' on," say Miz Sandy Claus. "You know yo' phthisic been develin' you, anyhow, and you'll git de chawley maw-buses sloppin' around in dis weather."

"No mind de tawk," say Sandy Claus. "Git me my umbrella and my overshoes. And you better git me a little somethin' to take along for a cradle gift, too, I reckon."

"You know hit ain't nothin' in de house for no cradle gift," say Miz Sandy Claus.

"Git somethin'," say Sandy Claus. "You got to give a new baby somethin', or else you got bad luck. Get me one er dem big red apples outn de kitchen."

"What kind er cradle gift is an apple?" say Miz Sandy Claus. "Don't you reckon dat baby git all de apples he want?"

"Git me de apple," say Sandy Claus. "Hit ain't much, one way you looks at hit. But f'm de way dat baby gonter look at de apple, hit'll be a heap."

So Sandy Claus got de apple and he lit out.

Well, when he got to Miss Mary's house ev'ybody was standin' around givin' de Poor Little Jesus presents. Fine presents. Made outn gold and silver and diamonds and silk, and all like dat. Dey had de presents stacked around dat baby so high you couldn't hardly see over 'em. So when ev'ybody seed old Sandy Claus come in dey looked to see what he brang. And when dey seed he didn't brang nothin' but a red apple, dey all laughed.

"Quick as dat boy grows up and gits to be de kaing," dey told him, "he gonter chop yo' haid off."

"No mind dat," say Sandy Claus. "Y'all jest stand back." And so he went up to de crib and he pushed away a handful er gold and silver and diamonds and stuff, and handed de Poor Little Jesus dat red apple. "Hyar, son," he say, "take dis old apple. See how she shines?"

And de Poor Little Jesus reached up and grabbed dat apple in bofe hands, and laughed jest as brash as you please!

Den Sandy Claus tuck and tickled him under de chin wid his before finger, and say, "Goodly-goodly-goodly." And de Poor Little Jesus laughed some more and he reached up and grabbed a fist full er old Sandy Claus' whiskers, and him and old Sandy Claus went round and round!

So about dat time, up stepped de Lawd. "I swear, old Sandy Claus," say de Lawd. "Betwix dat apple and dem whiskers, de Poor Little Jesus ain't had so much fun since he been bawn."

So Sandy Claus stepped back and bowed low and give de Lawd hy-dy, and say, "I didn't know ev'ybody was chiv-areein', or else I'd a stayed at home. I didn't had nothin' much to bring dis time, 'cause you see how hit's been dis year. De dry weather and de bull weevils got mighty nigh all de cotton, and de old lady been kind er puny—"

"Dat's all right, Sandy," say de Lawd. "Gold and silver have I a heap of. But verily you sho do know how to handle yo'se'f around de chilluns."

"Well, Lawd," say Sandy Claus, "I don't know much about chilluns. Me and de old lady raised up fou'teen. But she done most er de work. Me, I jest likes 'em and I manages to git along wid 'em."

"You sho do git along wid 'em good," say de Lawd.

"Hit's easy to do what you likes to do," say Sandy Claus.

"Well," say de Lawd, "hit might be somethin' in dat, too. But de trouble wid my world is, hit ain't enough people which likes to do de right thing. But you likes to do wid chilluns, and dat's what I needs. So stand still and shet yo' eyes whilst I passes a miracle on you."

So Sandy Claus stood still and shet his eyes, and de Lawd r'ared back and passed a miracle on him and say, "Old Sandy Claus, live forever, and make my chilluns happy."

So Sandy Claus opened his eyes and say, "Thank you kindly, Lawd. But do I got to keep 'em happy all de time? Dat's a purty big job. Hit'd be a heap er fun, but still and at de same time—"

"Yeah, I knows about chilluns, too," say de Lawd. "Chilluns got to fret and git in devilment ev'y now and den and git a whuppin' f'm dey maw, or else dey skin won't git loose so's dey kin grow. But you jest keep yo' eyes on 'em and make 'em all happy about once a year. How's dat?"

"Dat's fine," say Sandy Claus. "Hit'll be a heap er fun, too. What time er de year you speck I better make 'em happy, Lawd?"

"Christmas suit me," say de Lawd, "efn hit's all okay wid you."

"Hit's jest about right for me," say old Sandy Claus.

13

So ev'y since dat day and time old Sandy Claus been clawin' de chilluns on Christmas, and dat's on de same day dat de Poor Little Jesus got bawned. 'Cause dat's de way de Lawd runs things. O' cou'se de Lawd knowed hit wa'n't gonter be long before de Poor Little Jesus growed up and got to be a man. And when he done dat, all de grown fo'ks had him so's dey c'd moan they sins away and lay they burdens down on him, and git happy in they hearts. De Lawd made Jesus for de grown fo'ks. But de Lawd know de chilluns got to have some fun, too, so dat's how come hit's Sandy Claus and Christmas and all.

Roark Bradford

A Plantation Christmas

THE COCK CROWING for sunrise is scarcely over when the servants steal into the Big House on tiptoe so they can catch everybody there with a shouted "Christmas Gift!" before the kitchen fire is even started or the water put on to boil for the early morning coffee.

This is an old game. Everybody tries to catch everybody else and win an extra Christmas gift. Kind old maumas arrive before breakfast is over, fetching presents of new-laid eggs or fat pullet chickens tied by the legs, and their thanks for their gifts—aprons or sweets or fruits, or whatever else has been prepared for them—are expressed in the most charming, gracious words accompanied by the most graceful curtsies. Gentle old men fetch bags of peanuts or ears of popcorn or bottles of homemade syrup.

The cook forgets the heavy day's work ahead of him and joins heartily in the singing of Christmas spirituals out in the yard. The words of the beautiful songs are few, but their refrains repeated over and over in a thundering swirl unite us all in voice and faith and joy and help us to know that Christmas Day is the best day of our year.

And Christmas Week is our best week. Every night the big drum booms out with an invitation to a Christmas-tree party at some cabin. The Big Houses at the neighboring plantations are filled with fun until New Year's Day comes and ends the glad holiday season.

When nothing is left of the merrymaking but withered holly and faded mistletoe and the few red embers that still shine among the hickory ashes of the Christmas backlog, we rejoice that we are spared to pause and wonder over that strange miracle we call life.

Julia Peterkin

Christmas Gift

WELL, ONE CHRISTMAS time, God was goin' to Palatka. De Devil was in de neighborhood too and seen God goin' long de big road, so he jumped behind a stump and hid. Not dat he was skeered uh God, but he wanted to git a Christmas present outa God but he didn't wanta give God nothin'.

So he squatted down behind dis stump till God come along and then he jumped up and said, "Christmas Gift!"

God just looked back over his shoulder and said, "Take de East Coast," and kept on walkin'. And dat's why we got storms and skeeters— it's de Devil's property.

Zora Neale Hurston

The Legend
of the Black Madonna

ONCE UPON A time a magnificent church was being built in a certain city and there was need for one great stained glass window to go in a certain wall. The committee in charge felt that it would be wise to have artists from all over the world submit designs for this window, so they issued a general notice about their requirements and set a date when all sketches would be due. Many very famous painters entered drawings in the contest, but the one design on which all the committee agreed unanimously was made by an artist of unknown name and fame. The committee wrote him enthusiastically that they could not imagine any design which would better fill their requirements for the Church of the

Redeemer than his sketch entitled, "The Place Where the Young Child Lay." It was exactly what they wanted, so they commissioned him forthwith to go ahead with the work, the details of which they entrusted to him, warning him to have all in readiness for the dedication of the church on Christmas Eve.

The unknown artist was naturally very much elated at this fine opportunity to win fame and money, and he also saw in it a chance to work out a certain grudge which he had against all mankind—a grudge so deep and bitter that he thought of it day and night, and kept himself secluded in his attic studio rather than try to mix with the people whom he hated. He took the sketch that the committee had approved so enthusiastically and made certain little changes in it here and there with almost wicked delight. Then he called in his wife and his baby so that they could pose for the enlarged painting which he was to make.

Now it happened that his wife had been hanging out the family washing, and she came in wearing a shawl over her head and carrying the baby in the clothes basket. After she put down the basket she leaned over it, then looking up said gently: "Oh! the baby is sound asleep! If I pick him up he will awaken and cry. . . ."

"Don't pick him up," cried the artist. "Stay just where you are; that pose is perfect! Imagine that the clothes basket is a manger, that you are Mary, the mother of Jesus, and you have leaned over to see if He is sleeping, but now you have looked up because you hear the approach of someone. . . . Someone outside on camels: the three Wise Men . . . Way up here at the top of the canvas, see I shall paint the star that came and stood over where the young Child lay. . . . Stay perfectly still, dear . . . don't move . . . fine."

So the painter's wife kept the pose that he thought was so perfect and with quick, sure strokes he painted her as she knelt there. And it was a

far lovelier picture than he had planned to make it, because in the heart of his wife there was none of the bitter grudge that was in his heart. For when she looked down at her sleeping child, a great peace stole over her, and when she glanced up at her husband painting so rapidly and eagerly, a great contentment stole over her because at last his true talent had been discovered and the fame he so richly deserved was, at last, to come to him.

Then, too, as she knelt there in that quiet room, she began to realize who it was she represented . . . Mary, the mother of Jesus . . . the mother of the Saviour . . . ah, what a wonderful thing to feel that in the life of your little one the hopes of the whole world centered! She fell to wishing that her little boy could grow up with hands that would bless all mankind, with lips that could comfort those in trouble, as the Saviour's lips had always comforted the sorrowing. . . . Even as she brooded on the wonder of childhood, determined to train her boy in every Christ-like attitude, there came over her sweet, tired face a peace and beauty that was quite different from any that had ever been there before. And the artist gasped with surprise, catching the rare charm of her expression and painting her in hushed delight.

Yet, all the time, underneath his delight, the same old bitter hatred for mankind was working, and he kept saying to himself with fiendish glee, "The lovelier I make this picture, the better I can pay them back for all these years of hate and insult and injustice they have heaped upon me." So with one half of his soul he loved his wife, while the other half of his soul was steeped in unworthy mirth at the awful sensation he was going to create in that distant church on Christmas Eve.

Day after day the posing continued until finally the masterpiece was done, ready for the stained-glass factory workers; and here his difficulty lay, for if they discovered his secret, everything would be spoiled. He thought of a plan—a clever, secret plan that could not help but work out as he wished. The week before Christmas the various parts of the window arrived in that distant city where the new Church of the Redeemer was already completed. Trained workers began assembling the bits of glass, putting them in place, when a strange oversight bewildered them; neither the face nor arms of the Madonna and Child could be found high or low. The workmen were nearly frantic until the artist arrived and calmed their fears by saying that he had brought the missing parts of the window with him separately. It was a whim of his to put in the face and arms himself after all the rest of the window was ready.

"Just a sentiment of mine," he assured them. And when they discovered that he had mastered the correct process of fastening those extra pieces of glass in place, it was only natural that they agreed to his request. The whole building was fragrant with holly wreaths and pine; the florists who had been busily decorating pulpit and pillars and pews had departed; and the artist was alone to carry out his secret scheme.

With set lips and grim determination he climbed the ladder and with solder and lead and little instruments he fastened in place the lovely brooding face of the black Madonna, her tender protecting arms hovering over the sleeping Child, whose face and limbs he also attached in place.

"Now," hissed the artist vindictively, "now I have paid the world back for its treatment of me. Now all these Christian folks will be furious. They may even feel disgraced." When the time arrived for the dedication of the church, the artist slipped inconspicuously into a back pew, for as yet he was unknown to the committee. And just as he imagined, the entire congregation were looking up at his window with startled disapproving glances. There was whispering and nudging, and occasionally even an angry gesture. "Now, I am paying them back," grunted the artist with cold hate in his heart.

The beautiful dedication service proceeded as it had been planned, but when the last carol had been sung, and the benediction had been pronounced, groups of persons clustered in the aisles, and everybody was looking toward the window. "The face of that Madonna is certainly black," everybody was saying. "She looks exactly like a Negro. Even the baby looks like a Negro baby. The original sketch was not like this! Somebody has done us an injury. We cannot permit such a window in this magnificent church. . . ."

"Disgraceful! A black Madonna here? Of course not!"

The artist lurking behind a pillar chuckled with high glee. "Paying you back, all you fine white Christians, paying you back for all the years of insult that you have heaped on a poor Negro artist." And his black face grew hard with hatred and spite.

The midnight chimes rang out on the Christmas air, but the congregation had left the church with anything but goodwill in their hearts. The news of the marred window was telephoned all over the town, and although the service early Christmas morning was usually attended only by a few of the faithful souls, this year the capacity of the building was taxed, for everybody had come to see that black Madonna.

The minister was a very good man, and a just man, and a gentle man, and he had lain awake all night long, wondering, wondering, how he was ever going to preach the sermon he had announced from the text that was printed on that famous window, "In Him was life, and the life was the light of men." He had intended to build his whole sermon around the window; he had intended to point out the Christ Child and tell how the hopes of all mankind clustered around the place where the young child lay . . . but, now, should he point at that window? . . . at that black Madonna and Child? Seven o'clock found him walking into the dimly lighted pulpit with a miserable sinking in his heart as he saw the church packed with people, whose eyes were turned in one direction.

"This settles it," said the minister to himself. "I must preach about that window just as I had planned. But oh, Lord, help me to find the words to say." At last he rose and announced his text, "In Him was life, and the life was the light of men."

Suddenly the winter sun came blazing forth that Christmas morning with all the extra dazzle of a snowy day, and as its beams came breaking through the stained glass window, a gasp of sheer surprise spread through the church, for in that blaze of sunlight the Madonna's face was shining pure as an angel's and the little Christ Child's was a sheen of dazzling glory.

"In Him was life," he repeated, pointing upward, "and the life was the light of men." And inspired by the miracle of the transfigured black Madonna and Child he preached a sermon that marked a milestone in the life of every person present.

"Who are you and I to say we do not want a black Madonna in our church? In that great day of beginnings when the Lord God made man, did He specify, 'Let us make white man in our image?' No, 'let us make man.' And to some He gave black skins, to some yellow skins, to some brown skins, and to some white skins. He must have seen but little difference in these external colors, for it pleased Him to have an Africa with a hundred million black men; a China with four hundred million yellow men, and India with three hundred million brown men, and a Europe and America with several hundred million of white men. So, in deep humility, this Christmas Day I ask you—as the Saviour looks down into this Church of the Redeemer, who looks really black to his all-seeing gaze? That black Madonna? Or you and I with black consternation in our hearts because we feel the need of a Madonna with flesh the shade of our flesh? Oh, the conceit of us! The curious blackness of our hearts that cannot see God shine through those of another race or color. Have you forgotten the old familiar Bible story of how when the Lord God sent His little Son to earth, He did not choose a white-skinned mother for Him, but one whose cheeks were olive tan, a Jew? Let us then, this Christmas morning, be wise men bringing the gifts to the Saviour of all mankind, and, in the place where the young Child lay, let us put the most difficult present to give up—our race prejudice. For in Him is life, and the life is the light of all men—black men, and white men."

With faltering steps a dark-skinned man walked to the pulpit and placed in the minister's hand a package, explaining brokenly, "It is my Christmas present to this church which I have wronged so insanely and selfishly! See, here is the original white glass for the face of the Madonna and Child. I substituted the black glass myself. I wanted to prove to you what hypocrites you Christians were; that there was nothing to your religion but snobbish superiority. But you have shown me that I am wrong; you have shown me that I am color-blind, that in the sight of God Almighty there is neither black nor white—if His light shines through."

Then the congregation said: "We, too, have learned a lesson. Let us have the black Madonna in its place forever, so that our children and our children's children may see, each Sunday, how the light that came to earth with the Christ Child is indeed the light of the world, shining through the faces of God's earth family, no matter what the color of the face may be!" And together they sang: "Praise God from whom all blessings flow," and went out with a new appreciation of the angel's message: "Peace on earth among men and women of goodwill" one toward another.

Margaret T. Applegarth

Goat Comes
to the Christmas Party

HURRY! HURRY! HURRY!" said Gran'ma to Araminta. "It's time to go to the party."

"Hurry! Hurry! Hurry!" said Araminta to Jerome Anthony. "It's time to go to the party."

Christmas had come to the country, and there was going to be a party at the schoolhouse. Everybody was going, so Araminta and Jerome Anthony and Gran'ma had to hurry, else they'd be late and miss something.

"I wish Goat could go to the party," said Araminta, shaking her head sadly. "It seems a shame that Goat can't have any Christmas at all."

"Goats don't have Christmas," laughed Jerome Anthony. "Whatever would Goat do at a party?"

"Hurry! Hurry! Hurry!" said Gran'ma, looking at her watch.

So they put on their hats and coats and mittens. They tied their scarves under their chins, and they started out. It was cold, so they walked fast and it didn't take any time to get to the schoolhouse. If they hadn't hurried they might have been late, for the party was just about to begin.

Everyone was there sitting on the school benches that were pushed back against the wall of the room. The little Christmas tree was there standing straight and tall in the front of the room. The beautiful paper chains and popcorn strings were there *on* the Christmas tree just where they belonged. And over in one corner was a table filled with cakes and lemonade and candy, for of course a party isn't a party without good things to eat.

"Where is Gran'pa?" asked Jerome Anthony, turning around in his seat. "I'm afraid Gran'pa is going to be late."

"Don't you worry," smiled Gran'ma. "Gran'pa will get here. He has a surprise for you."

"Surprise!" whispered Araminta, very excited. Then her face was sad. "Oh dear, I do wish Goat could be here for the surprise."

Just then there was a little noise at the back door and everyone turned around. Well, you can't imagine what they saw! Santa Claus! There he was in a red suit with white trimmings, and a red hat with a white tassel. And he had the reddest face you've ever seen, with a long white beard at the bottom of it.

"Oh! Oh!" yelled everybody.

"Shh-h-h," whispered everybody.

For Santa Claus had somebody with him. This somebody was black and white with long floppy ears and a short stumpy tail. This somebody had long curly horns that looked very much like the branches of a tree. This somebody was hitched to a new green wagon. Yes, you've guessed it. Santa Claus had a reindeer with him, and this reindeer was pulling a wagon full of toys!

"Oh! Oh! Oh!" yelled everybody.

"Shh-h-h-h!" whispered everybody.

For Santa Claus and the reindeer were starting up the aisle toward the Christmas tree. They walked along steadily, until they came to the bench where Jerome Anthony and Araminta were sitting, and then something very queer happened. That reindeer lifted his stumpy tail; he shook his head and his ears went flip-flop.

"GOAT!" yelled Araminta, jumping up and down. "Goat has come to the party!"

We can't be sure whether it was Araminta yelling or the sight of the Christmas tree, but anyway, just then that Santa Claus reindeer stopped acting like a reindeer and began acting like a goat instead. He butted Santa Claus out of the way. He broke loose from his wagon. He began *eating* the Christmas tree!

"Hey! Watch out!" said Santa Claus, falling against one of the benches. When he got up, that red face with the long white beard had fallen off.

"Gran'pa!" yelled Jerome Anthony. "Gran'pa got here after all!"

We can't be sure whether it was Jerome Anthony yelling or the sight of that goat eating the Christmas tree, but anyway, Santa Claus stopped acting like Santa Claus and began to act like Gran'pa instead. He grabbed hold of Goat. But every time he tried to get Goat to stop eating the popcorn off the tree, Goat rared up and butted him against the benches again.

"Let me help," said Araminta, jumping up. "I can manage that Goat."

She grabbed Goat by his bridle and started to lead him away before he ruined the tree. But just then Goat caught sight of that table full of cakes and candy and lemonade, and he pulled toward that. Now when goats see something that they want to eat, you know how hard it is to keep them away from it. Araminta pulled and pulled, but it didn't do any good. Goat kept on getting closer and closer to that table of good food.

"Oh! Oh! Oh!" everybody yelled. They didn't want all their party refreshments to be eaten up.

"Shh-h-h!" everybody whispered, because it looked as if Jerome Anthony was going to do something about it.

He took two pieces of chocolate cake from the table and he held them out to Goat.

"Here, Goat!" he said.

Goat looked at that cake held out for him to eat; he reared up on his hind legs and shook those pretend-like reindeer horns off his own short horns; then he ran after Jerome Anthony! Jerome Anthony ran down the middle of the schoolhouse, holding that cake so Goat could see it. Jerome Anthony ran out the door, with Goat after him.

"Humph!" said Araminta, taking a deep breath, "I shouldn't have worried about Goat not having any Christmas. He had more than anybody else."

Gran'pa put on his red face with the white whiskers and there he was—a Santa Claus again. "Merry Christmas!" he laughed, as he began to give out the toys. "Merry Christmas!" yelled everybody.

"Maa-aa! Maa-a-a!" came Goat's voice from the schoolhouse yard.

But nobody opened the door to let him in.

Eva Knox Evans

New Relations and Duties

MY TERM OF service with Edward Covey expired on Christmas Day, 1834. I gladly enough left him, although he was by this time as gentle as a lamb. My home for the year 1835 was already secured, my next master selected. There was always more or less excitement about the changing hands, but determined to fight my way, I had become somewhat reckless and cared little into whose hands I fell. The report got abroad that I was hard to whip; that I was guilty of kicking back, and that, though generally a good-natured Negro, I sometimes "got the devil in me." These sayings were rife in Talbot County and distinguished me among my servile brethren. Slaves would sometimes fight with one another, and even die at one another's hands, but there were very few who were not held in awe by a white man. Trained from the cradle up to think and feel that their masters were superiors and invested with a sort of sacredness, there were few who could rise above the control which that sentiment exercised. I had freed myself from it, and the thing was known. One bad sheep will spoil a whole flock. I was a bad sheep. I hated slavery, slaveholders, and all pertaining to them; and I did not fail to inspire others with the same feeling wherever and whenever opportunity was presented. This made me a marked lad among the slaves, and a suspected one among slaveholders. A knowledge also of my ability to read and write got pretty widely spread, which was very much against me.

The days between Christmas Day and New Year's were allowed the slaves as holidays. During these days all regular work was suspended, and there was nothing to do but keep fires and look after the stock. We regarded this time as our own by the grace of our masters, and we therefore used it or abused it as we pleased. Those who had families at a distance were expected to visit them and spend with them the entire week. The younger slaves or the unmarried ones were expected to see to the animals and attend to incidental duties at home. The holidays were variously spent. The sober, thinking, industrious ones would employ themselves in manufacturing corn brooms, mats, horse collars, and baskets, and some of these were very well made. Another class spent their time in hunting opossums, coons, rabbits, and other game. But the majority spent the holidays in sports, ball-playing, wrestling, boxing, running, foot races, dancing, and drinking whiskey; and this latter mode was generally most agreeable to their masters. A slave who would work during the holidays was thought by his master undeserving of holidays. There was in this simple act of continued work an accusation against slaves, and a slave could not help thinking that if he made three dollars during the holidays he might make three hundred during the year. Not to be drunk during the holidays was disgraceful.

The fiddling, dancing, and "jubilee beating" was carried on in all directions. This latter performance was strictly Southern. It supplied the place of violin or other musical instruments and was played so easily that almost every farm had its "Juba" beater. The performer improvised as he beat the instrument, marking the words as he sang so as to have them fall pat with the movement of his hands. Once in a while among a mass of nonsense and wild frolic, a sharp hit was given to the meanness of slaveholders.

Take the following for example:

> *We raise de wheat,*
> *Dey gib us de corn;*
> *We bake de bread,*
> *Dey gib us de crust;*
> *We sif de meal,*
> *Dey gib us de huss;*
>
> *We peel de meat,*
> *Dey gib us de skin;*
> *And dat's de way*
> *Dey take us in.*

This is not a bad summary of the palpable injustice and fraud of slavery, giving, as it does, to the lazy and idle the comforts which God designed should be given solely to the honest laborer. But to the holidays. Judging from my own observation and experience, I believe those holidays were among the most effective means in the hands of slaveholders of keeping down the spirit of insurrection among the slaves.

Frederick Douglass

34

Anxious Days and
Sleepless Nights

THE COMING OF Christmas, that first year of our residence in Alabama, gave us an opportunity to get a further insight into the real life of the people. The first thing that reminded us that Christmas had arrived was the "foreday" visits of scores of children rapping at our doors, asking for "Chris'mus gifts! Chris'mus gifts!" Between the hours of two o'clock and five o'clock in the morning I presume that we must have had a half-hundred such calls. This custom prevails throughout this portion of the South today.

During the days of slavery it was a custom quite generally observed throughout all the Southern states to give the colored people a week of holiday at Christmas, or to allow the holiday to continue as long as the "yule log" lasted. The male members of the race, and often the female members, were expected to get drunk. We found that for a whole week the colored people in and around Tuskegee dropped work the day before Christmas, and that it was difficult to get anyone to perform any service from the time they stopped work until after the New Year. Persons who at other times did not use strong drink thought it quite the proper thing to indulge in it rather freely during the Christmas week. There was a widespread hilarity, and a free use of guns, pistols, and gunpowder generally. The sacredness of the season seemed to have been almost wholly lost sight of.

During this first Christmas vacation I went some distance from the town to visit the people on one of the large plantations. In their poverty and ignorance it was pathetic to see their attempts to get joy out of the season that in most parts of the country is so sacred and so dear to the heart. In one cabin I noticed that all that the five children had to remind them of the coming of Christ was a single bunch of firecrackers, which they had divided among them. In another cabin, where there were at least a half-dozen persons, they had only ten cents' worth of ginger cakes, which had been bought in the store the day before. In another family they had only a few pieces of sugarcane. In still another cabin I found nothing but a new jug of cheap, mean whiskey, which the husband and wife were making free use of, notwithstanding the fact that the husband was one of the local ministers. In a few instances I found that the people had gotten hold of some brightly colored cards that had been designed for advertising purposes and were making the most of those. In other homes some member of the family had bought a new pistol. In the majority of cases there was nothing to be seen in the cabin to remind one of the coming of the Saviour, except that the people had ceased work in the fields and were lounging about their homes. At night, during Christmas week, they usually had what they called a "frolic" in some cabin on the plantation. This meant a kind of rough dance, where there was likely to be a good deal of whiskey used, and where there might be some shooting or cutting with razors.

While I was making this Christmas visit I met an old colored man who was one of the numerous local preachers, who tried to convince me, from the experience Adam had in the Garden of Eden, that God had cursed all labor, and that, therefore, it was a sin for any man to work. For that reason this man sought to do as little work as possible. He seemed at that time to be supremely happy, because he was living, as he expressed it, through one week that was free from sin.

In the school we made a special effort to teach our students the meaning of Christmas and to give them lessons in its proper observance. In this we have been successful to a degree that makes me feel safe in saying that the season now has a new meaning, not only through all that immediate region, but, in a measure, wherever our graduates have gone.

At the present time one of the most satisfactory features of the Christmas and Thanksgiving seasons at Tuskegee is the unselfish and beautiful way in which our graduates and students spend their time in administering to the comfort and happiness of others, especially the unfortunate. Not long ago some of our young men spent a holiday in rebuilding a cabin for a helpless colored woman who is about seventy-five years old. At another time I remember that I made it known in chapel, one night, that a very poor student was suffering from cold, because he needed a coat. The next morning two coats were sent to my office for him.

Booker T. Washington

Chrismus Is A-Comin'

Bones a-gittin' achy,
Back a-feelin' col',
Han's a-growin' shaky,
Jes' lak I was ol'.
Fros' erpon de meddah
Lookin' mighty white;
Snowdrops lak a feddah
Slippin' down at night.
Jes' keep t'ings a-hummin'
Spite o' fros' an' showahs,
Chrismus is a-comin'
An' all de week is ouahs.

Little mas' a-axin',
"Who is Santy Claus?"
Meks it kin' o' taxin'
Not to brek de laws.
Chillun's pow'ful tryin'
To a pusson's grace
W'en dey go a-pryin'
Right on th'oo you' face
Down ermong yo' feelin's;
Jes' 'pears lak dat you
Got to change you' dealin's
So's to tell 'em true.

An' my pickaninny—
Dreamin' in his sleep!
Come hyeah, Mammy Jinny,
Come an' tek a peep.
Ol' Mas' Bob an' Missis
In dey house up daih
Got no chile lak dis is,
D' ain't none anywhaih.
Sleep, my little lammy,
Sleep, you little limb,
He do' know whut mammy
Done saved up fu' him.

Dey'll be banjo pickin',
Dancin' all night thoo.
Dey'll be lots o' chicken,
Plenty tukky, too.
Drams to wet yo' whistles
So's to drive out chills.
Whut I keer fu' drizzles
Fallin' on de hills?
Jes' keep t'ings a-hummin'
Spite o' col' an' showahs,
Chrismus day's a-comin',
An' all de week is ouahs.

Paul Laurence Dunbar

Speakin' o' Christmas

Breezes blowin' middlin' brisk,
Snowflakes thro' the air a-whisk,
Fallin' kind o' soft an' light,
Not enough to make things white,
But jest sorter siftin' down
So's to cover up the brown
Of the dark world's rugged ways
'N' make things look like holidays.
Not smoothed over, but jest specked,
Sorter strainin' fur effect,

An' not quite a-gittin' through
What it started in to do.
Mercy sakes! it does seem queer
Christmas day is 'most nigh here.
Somehow it don't seem to me
Christmas like it used to be—
Christmas with its ice an' snow,
Christmas of the long ago.
You could feel its stir an' hum
Weeks an' weeks before it come;
Somethin' in the atmosphere
Told you when the day was near,
Didn't need no almanacs;
That was one o' Nature's fac's.
Every cottage decked out gay—
Cedar wreaths an' holly spray—
An' the stores, how they were drest,
Tinsel tell you couldn't rest;
Every winder fixed up pat,
Candy canes, an' things like that,
Noah's arks, an' guns, an' dolls,
An' all kinds o' fol-de-rols.
Then with frosty bells a-chime,
Slidin' down the hills o' time,
Right amidst the fun an' din
Christmas come a-bustlin' in,
Raised his cheery voice to call
Out a welcome to us all;
Hale and hearty, strong an' bluff,

That was Christmas, sure enough.
Snow knee-deep an' coastin' fine,
Frozen millponds all ashine,
Seemin' jest to lay in wait,
Beggin' you to come an' skate.
An' you'd git your gal an' go
Stumpin' cheerily thro' the snow,
Feelin' pleased an' skeert an' warm
'Cause she had a-holt yore arm.
Why, when Christmas come in, we
Spent the whole glad day in glee,
Havin' fun an' feastin' high
An' some courtin' on the sly.
Bustin' in some neighbor's door
An' then suddenly, before
He could give his voice a lift,
Yellin' at him, "Christmas gift."
Now sich things are never heard,
"Merry Christmas" is the word.
But it's only change o' name,
An' means givin' jest the same.
There's too many new-styled ways
Now about the holidays.
I'd jest like once more to see
Christmas like it used to be!

Paul Laurence Dunbar

Christmas Carol

Ring out, ye bells!
All Nature swells
With gladness of the wondrous story—
The world was lorn,
But Christ is born
To change our sadness into glory.

Sing, earthlings, sing!
Tonight a King
Hath come from heaven's high throne to bless us.
The outstretched hand
O'er all the land
Is raised in pity to caress us.

Come at His call;
Be joyful all;
Away with mourning and with sadness!
The heavenly choir
With holy fire
Their voices raise in songs of gladness.

45

The darkness breaks
And Dawn awakes,
Her cheeks suffused with youthful blushes.
The rocks and stones
In holy tones
Are singing sweeter than the thrushes.

Then why should we
In silence be,
When Nature lends her voice to praises;
When heaven and earth
Proclaim the truth
Of Him for whom that lone star blazes?

No, be not still,
But with a will
Strike all your harps and set them ringing;
On hill and heath
Let every breath
Throw all its power into singing!

Paul Laurence Dunbar

46

A Little Christmas Basket

De win' is hollahin' "Daih you" to de shuttahs an' de fiah,
De snow's a-sayin' "Got you" to de groun',
Fu' de wintah weathah's come widout a-askin' ouah desiah,
An' he's laughin' in his sleeve at whut he foun';
Fu' dey ain't nobody ready wid dey fuel er dey food,
An' de money bag look timid lak, fu' sho',
So we want ouah Chrismus sermon, but we'd lak it ef you could
Leave a little Chrismus basket at de do'.

Wha's de use o' tellin' chillen 'bout a Santy er a Nick,
An' de sto'ies dat a body allus tol'?
When de harf is gray wid ashes an' you hasn't got a stick
Fu' to warm dem when dey little toes is col'?
Wha's de use o' preachin' 'ligion to a man dat's sta'ved to def,
An' a-tellin' him de Mastah will pu'vide?
Ef you want to tech his feelin's, save yo' sermons an' yo' bref,
Tek a little Chrismus basket by yo' side.

'T ain't de time to open Bibles an' to lock yo' cellah do',
'T ain't de time to talk o' bein' good to men;
Ef you want to preach a sermon ez you nevah preached befo',
Preach dat sermon wid a shoat er wid er hen;
Bein' good is heap sight bettah den a-dallyin' wid sin,
An' dey ain't nobody roun' dat knows it mo',
But I t'ink dat 'ligion's sweeter w'en it kind o' mixes in
Wid a little Chrismus basket at de do'.

Paul Laurence Dunbar

Through the Holly Wreath

I peeped once through a holly wreath.
What do you think I saw?
The round, red face of Santa Claus
With cherries in his jaw.

His nose was just a great bonbon,
His curls coconut shreds.
His lips were smiling, I could see,
In holly berry reds.

Effie Lee Newsome

49

The Magi Call Him King

A CHRISTMAS SONG

O shepherds, while you watch your flocks
The Wise Men watch His Star,
The Magi who come worshiping
With incense from afar.

Know, shepherds, you who find the place,
So humble, where He lies,
The Magi ride with splendid gifts
Under the midnight skies.

Oh you of sheep, who seek the fold
Of Him the angels sing,
Though He be called "Good Shepherd" too,
The Magi call Him KING.

Effie Lee Newsome

Carol of the Brown King

Of the three Wise Men
Who came to the King,
One was a brown man,
So they sing.

Of the three Wise Men
Who followed the Star,
One was a brown king
From afar.

They brought fine gifts
Of spices and gold
In jeweled boxes
Of beauty untold.

Unto His humble
Manger they came
And bowed their heads
In Jesus' name.

Three Wise Men,
One dark like me—
Part of His
Nativity.

Langston Hughes

Kid Stuff

The wise guys
tell me
that Christmas
is Kid Stuff...
Maybe they've got
something there—

Two thousand years ago
three wise guys
chased a star
across a continent
to bring
frankincense and myrrh
to a Kid
born in a manger
with an idea in his head...

And as the bombs
crash
all over the world
today
the real wise guys
know
that we've all
got to go chasing stars
again
in the hope
that we can get back
some of that
Kid Stuff
born two thousand years ago—

Frank Horne
December, 1942

On a Pallet of Straw

They did not travel in an airplane,
They did not travel by car,
They did not travel on a streamline train.
They traveled on foot from afar,
They traveled on foot from afar.

They did not seek for a fine hotel,
They did not seek an inn,
They did not seek a bright motel.
They sought a cattle bin,
They sought a cattle bin.

Who were these travelers on the road?
And where were they going? And why?
They were Three Wise Men who came from the East,
And they followed a star in the sky,
A star in the sky.

What did they find when they got to the barn?
What did they find near the stall?
What did they find on a pallet of straw?
They found there the Lord of all!
They found the Lord of all!

Langston Hughes

The Peppermint Candy March

The peppermint candy march
Went gaily on up the street,
All dressed in white and red,
Each with a lime-drop head,
And bonbons like brown shoes for feet.

Each band man blew a little coil
Made of the silver wrapping foil.
I hope they got far on their way,
Because at ending of the day,
I'm sure there isn't any doubt
The hungry mice would all come out.

Effie Lee Newsome

Shepherd's Song at Christmas

Look there at the star!
I, among the least,
Will arise and take
A journey to the East.
But what shall I bring
As a present for the King?
What shall I bring to the Manger?

I will bring a song,
A song that I will sing,
A song for the King
In the Manger.

Watch out for my flocks,
Do not let them stray.
I am going on a journey
Far, far away.
But what shall I bring
As a present for the Child?
What shall I bring to the Manger?

I will bring a lamb.
Gentle, meek, and mild,
A lamb for the Child
In the Manger.

I'm just a shepherd boy,
Very poor I am—
But I know there is
A King in Bethlehem.
What shall I bring
As a present just for Him?
What shall I bring to the Manger?

I will bring my heart
And give my heart to Him.
I will give my heart
To the Manger.

Langston Hughes

The Christmas Story

Tell again the Christmas story:
Christ is born in all His glory!
Baby laid in manger, dark
Lighting centuries with the spark
Of innocence that is the Child
Trusting all within His smile.

Tell again the Christmas story
With the halo of His glory:
Halo born of humbleness
By the breath of cattle blest,
By the poverty of stall
Where a bed of straw is all,

By a door closed at the inn
Where only men of means get in,
By a door closed to the poor
Christ is born on earthen floor
In a stable with no lock—
Yet kingdoms tremble at the shock
Of infant King in swaddling clothes
At an address no one knows
Because there is no painted sign—
Nothing but a star divine,
Nothing but a halo bright
About His young head in the night,
Nothing but the wondrous light
Of innocence that is the Child
Trusting all within His smile.

Mary's Son of golden star:
Wise Men journey from afar!

Mary's Son in manger born:
Music of an Angel's horn!

Mary's Son in straw and glory:
Wonder of the Christmas story!

Langston Hughes

On a Christmas Night

In Bethlehem on a Christmas night
All around the Child shone a holy light.
All around His head was a halo bright
On a Christmas night.

"We have no room," the innkeeper called,
So the glory fell where the cows were stalled,
But among the guests were Three Kings who called
On a Christmas night.

How can it be such a light shines here
In this humble stable once cold and drear?
Oh, the Child has come to bring good cheer
On a Christmas night!

And what is the name of the little One?
His name is Jesus—He's God's own Son.
Be happy, happy, everyone
On a Christmas night!

Langston Hughes

An Anonymous Verse

FROM A PUERTO RICAN CHRISTMAS CARD

Lady Santa Ana
Why does the Child cry?

*About an orange He's lost
and cannot spy.*

Tell Him not to cry
For I have two—

One for the Child
And one for you.

*Translated from the Spanish
by Langston Hughes*

Every Man Heart Lay Down

Long time past
Before you papa live
Before him papa live
Before him pa's papa live—

Long time past
Before them big tree live
Before them big tree's papa live—
That time God live.

And God look on the world
What He done make
And Him heart no lay down.
And He walk about in the town
To see the people

And He sit down in the palaver house
To know the people
And He vex too much.
And God say
>"Nev mind.
>The people no hear My Word
>The people no walk My way
>Nev mind.
>I going break the world and lose the people
>I going make the day dark
>And the night I going make hot.
>I going make water that side where land belong
>And land that side where water belong.
>And I going make a new country
>And make a new people."

Now this time
God's one small boy—Him small pican—hear God's Word
And the pican grieve for people
So he go fore God's face
And make talk for him Pa.
>"Pa, I come for beg You," so he say
>"I come for beg You,
>Don't break the world
>What You done make.
>Don't lose the people
>What You done care for.
>I beg You
>Make it I go

I talk to people
I walk with people
Bye-m-bye they savvy the way."

And the pican go down softly softly
And hold God's foot.
So God look on Him small boy
And Him heart be soft again
And God say
    "Aye My son,
    When you beg Me so
    I no can vex.
    Left Me now, but hear Me good:
    If you go you must be born like a man
    And you must live like a man
    And you must have hurt and have hunger.
    And hear Me good:
    Men will hate you
    And they will flog you
    And bye-m-bye they will kill you
    And I no going put My hand there."

And the pican say
    "I agree!"

And bye-m-bye God call Mary
To be Ma for the pican
Now Mary be new wife for Joseph

And Joseph ain't touch Mary self
So first time Joseph vex.
But God say
      "Nev mind, Joseph,
        This be God palaver."
And Joseph heart lay down.

And God see one king who try for do good
For all him people
And God say
      "Ahah, Now I send My son
        For be new king."
And God send star to call the king.

And in a far country
God hear a wise man call Him name
And God say to the wise man
      "I send My son to be new wise man,
        Go now with the star."
And the star call
And the wise man follow.
And by the waterside
Men lay down for take rest
And they hear fine music in the sky
Like all the stars make song,
And they fear.
And all the dark make bright like day
And the water shine like fire
And no man can savvy
And they hearts turn over.

But God's angel come
And God's angel say
        "Make glad, all people,
        God's pican be born in Bethlehem."
And the people say "Oh."

And the wise man and the king
And the country people come to Bethlehem
And the star come low and stop.
But when they go for mansion house
The star no be there.
And when they go for Big Man's house
The star no be there.
And bye-m-bye when they go for hotel
The star no be there gain—
But the wise man say
        "Ahah, the star be by the small house
        Where cattle sleep!"
And it was so.

And they find Joseph and Mary
And the small small pican
Fold up in country cloth
And the king bring gold for gift
And the wise man bring fine oil
And the country people bring new rice.

And they look on the God pican
And every man heart lay down.

Lorenz Graham

The Stable

When midnight came
and the Child's first cry arose,
a hundred beasts awakened
and the stable became alive.

And drawing near they came
reaching out toward the Child
a hundred eager necks
like a forest swaying.

An ox whose eyes were tender
as though filled with dew,
lowered its head to breathe
quietly in His face.

Against Him rubbed a lamb
with the softest of soft fleece,
and two baby goats squatted,
licking His hands.

The walls of the stable
unnoticed were covered
with pheasants and with geese
and cocks and with blackbirds.

The pheasants flew down
and swept over the Child
tails of many colors;

while the geese with wide bills
smoothed His pallet of straw;
and a swarm of blackbirds
became a veil rising and falling
above the new born.

The Virgin, confused among such horns
and whiteness of breathing,
fluttered hither and yon
unable to pick up her Child.

Joseph arrived laughing
to help her in her confusion,
and the upset stable was like
a forest in the wind.

Gabriela Mistral
Translated from the Spanish
by Langston Hughes

Indian Christmas

Mother with no Christmas gifts,
large or small, anywhere,
dreaming at midnight,
I give my child quite bare.

High amid harsh stubble
in the air of the Andes rare,
the only gift I have to give
is my child quite bare.

The wind from La Puna
that cries so sharply there,
has no cry like the cry
of my child quite bare.

God watches over all.
By Him, to do my share,
On Holy Night I offer
my child quite bare.

Gabriela Mistral
Translated from the Spanish
by Langston Hughes

Go Tell It on the Mountain

Go tell it on the mountain,
Over the hills and everywhere;
Go tell it on the mountain,
That Jesus Christ is born.

When I was a seeker,
I sought both night and day,
I asked the Lord to help me,
And He showed me the way.

He made me a watchman
Upon a city wall,
And if I am a Christian,
I am the least of all.

Go tell it on the mountain,
Over the hills and everywhere;
Go tell it on the mountain,
That Jesus Christ is born.

Negro spiritual

Wasn't That a Mighty Day

Wasn't that a mighty day
When Jesus Christ was born?
Star shone in the East,
Star shone in the East,
Star shone in the East
When Jesus Christ was born!

Negro spiritual

The Virgin Mary Had
a Baby Boy

The Virgin Mary had a baby boy,
The Virgin Mary had a baby boy,
The Virgin Mary had a baby boy,
And they said His name was Jesus.
He come from the glory,
He come from the glorious kingdom!
Oh, yes, believer!
He come from the glory,
He come from the glorious kingdom!

Negro spiritual

What You Gonna Name That Pretty Little Baby?

Oh, Mary, what you gonna name
That pretty little baby?
Glory, glory, glory
To the newborn King!
Some will call Him one thing,
But I think I'll call Him Jesus.
Glory, glory, glory
To the newborn King!
Some will call Him one thing,
But I think I'll say Emanuel.
Glory, glory, glory
To the newborn King!

Negro spiritual

Rise Up, Shepherd, and Follow

There's a star in the East
On Christmas morn.
Rise up, shepherd, and follow!
It'll lead to the place
Where the Saviour's born.
Rise up, shepherd, and follow!
If you take good heed
To the angel's words and
Rise up, shepherd, and follow,
You'll forget your flocks,
You'll forget your herds.
Rise up, shepherd, and follow!
Leave your sheep, leave your lambs,
Rise up, shepherd, and follow!
Leave your ewes, leave your rams,
Rise up, shepherd, and follow!
Follow the Star of Bethlehem,
Rise up, shepherd, and follow!

Negro spiritual

God's Christmas Tree

We are all a part of the selfsame tree—
The bark and the limbs are all akin,
And the leaves are expressive of something within.
The roots deep down from the good brown earth
Give forth their little or their great worth.

Blood of one red blood are we,
Like the sap that flows from the selfsame tree,
From the fountain of life, superb and free;
All men are a branch of the Mother Tree,
Who loves and nurtures humanity.

Eve Lynn
(Evelyn C. Reynolds)

78

Under the Mistletoe

I did not know she'd take it so,
Or else I'd never dared:
Although the bliss was worth the blow,
I did not know she'd take it so.
She stood beneath the mistletoe
So long I thought she cared;
I did not know she'd take it so,
Or else I'd never dared.

Countee Cullen

The Black Madonna

Not as the white nations
know thee
O Mother!

But swarthy of cheek
and full-lipped as the
child races are.

Yet thou are she,
  the Immaculate Maid,
    and none other,

Crowned in the stable
  at Bethlehem,
    hailed of the star.

See where they come,
  thy people,
    so humbly appealing,

From the ancient lands
  where the olden faiths
    had birth.

Tired dusky hands
  uplifting for thy
    healing.

Pity them, Mother,
  the untaught
    of earth.

Albert Rice

Otto

It's Christmas Day. I did not get
The presents that I hoped for. Yet,
It is not nice to frown or fret.

To frown or fret would not be fair.
My Dad must never know I care
It's hard enough for him to bear.

Gwendolyn Brooks

82

Christmas Recipes

from the "Big House"

and the Cabin

THE SLAVE COOKS were famous for their rich and varied foods. The most renowned were the female slaves who cooked solely for "Ol' Massa" and his family in the "Big House." The slave owner took pride as the fame of his table spread throughout the immediate area. The slave cook was valued highly, and she was justifiably proud of her work. It was not at all unusual to find a rather autocratic slave cook, who held sway over the kitchen helpers, enjoyed a status higher than that of the field hand, and was given special liberties by her owner. Pride in her work, and the subsequent pleasing of her master, insured a continuation of the slave cook's favorable status. She further utilized this freedom by using a lavish hand when working with choice cuts of meat, thick cream, spices, and other ingredients.

Not so lucky was the slave who cooked for her own family. To her went the least desirable of foodstuffs—the head, feet, and tail of the pig—while the choice hams and cuts of meat suitable for roasting went to the "Big House." The slave family cook, however, used imagination, and with the ingredients at hand, created dishes to provide a welcome variety to the monotony of a diet composed of the inexpensive, bulky foodstuffs allocated by her owner. Both cooks used ingredients native to the region: unrefined sugar, molasses, cornmeal, nutmeats—some plentiful, some available only in limited quantities, but all used with ingenuity. Regardless of the location of the kitchen, the slave cook passed on recipes by word of mouth. Few recipes were ever written down.

The recipes that I have included here represent some from the "Big House" and some from the cabin. Most of the recipes came to me from my grandmother; others are family recipes given to me by friends. The recipes were written down only recently; formerly they were verbal instructions and contained such picturesque directions as, "Use a piece of butter the size of your fist"; "Throw a handful of rice in the pot"; "Use a smidgen of sage"; "Punch holes in the top of biscuit dough with a five-tine' fork." The recipes have been slightly adapted to conform with modern cookery, but I have attempted to retain their unique character.

Most of these recipes were used only for Christmas week, a time for the most lavish cooking of the year. Nuts, gathered in the fall of the year, were saved especially for this time. My grandmother and her contemporaries started their cooking the week before Christmas; then, freed from the labor of the fields, time would be spent more happily in the cookshed. Working hard, no good cook would ever let Christmas "catch" her with less than six cakes and a dozen assorted pies, prepared and waiting in the "safe" for Christmas guests. The "safe" was a fly-proof cupboard with shelves, the top doors of which were made of tin, punctured in a perforated design. The perforations served as vents to let in cool air to preserve the food. Into the "safe" at Christmas week also went tea cakes, baked chicken, roast wild turkey, duck, and goose.

At Christmas time, tea cakes were made in abundance. These simple nutmeg-flavored sugar cookies were standard equipment in any "safe." They were useful for passing out on the call of "Christmas Gif'!" Other times of the year, tea cakes were made sparingly as a simple dessert, for my grandmother recalled that no long journey was ever made without taking along "a flour sack half-full of tea cakes."

Knowing now a little of the background of cooking during the days of slavery, I hope that the reader who uses these recipes will feel some of the gaiety and enjoyment felt by others in festive, toil-free Christmas weeks of long ago.

Biblical References
for SCRIPTURE CAKE

I. KINGS *4:22*

And Solomon's provision for one day was thirty measures of fine FLOUR, *and threescore measures of meal.*

I. CORINTHIANS *5:6*

Your glorying is not good. Know ye not that a little LEAVEN *leaveneth the whole lump?*

LEVITICUS *2:13*

And every oblation of thy meat offering shalt thou season with SALT; . . . *with all thine offerings thou shalt offer salt.*

I. KINGS *10:10*

And she gave the king an hundred and twenty talents of gold, and of SPICES *very great store, and precious stones: there came no more such abundance of spices as these which the queen of Sheba gave to king Solomon.*

JUDGES *5:25*

He asked water, and she gave him milk; she brought forth BUTTER *in a lordly dish.*

JEREMIAH *6:20*

To what purpose cometh there to me incense from Sheba, and the SWEET CANE *from a far country?*

ISAIAH *10:14*

And my hand hath found as a nest the riches of the people: and as one gathereth EGGS *that are left, have I gathered all the earth; . . .*

GENESIS *24:17*

And the servant ran to meet her, and said, Let me, I pray thee, drink a little WATER *of thy pitcher.*

EXODUS *3:8*

And I am come down to deliver them out of the hand of the Egyptians, and to bring them up out of that land unto a good land . . . flowing with milk and HONEY; . . .

I. SAMUEL *30:12*

And they gave him a piece of a cake of FIGS, *and two clusters of* RAISINS: *and when he had eaten, his spirit came to him: for he had eaten no bread, nor drunk any water, three days and three nights.*

GENESIS *43:11*

And their father Israel said unto them, If it must be so now, do this; take of the best fruits in the land in your vessels, and carry down the man a present, a little balm, and a little honey, spices, and myrrh, NUTS, *and almonds.*

PROVERBS *23:13*

Withhold not correction from the child: for if thou BEATEST *him with the rod, he shall not die.*

NOTE: *Emphasis within each verse is compiler's.*

SCRIPTURE CAKE

(10–12 servings)

I. KINGS *4:22*	3½ cups sifted flour
I. CORINTHIANS *5:6*	2 teaspoons baking powder
LEVITICUS *2:13*	½ teaspoon salt
I. KINGS *10:10*	¼ teaspoon nutmeg
Ibid.	¼ teaspoon cinnamon
Ibid.	¼ teaspoon allspice
JUDGES *5:25*	1 cup butter
JEREMIAH *6:20*	2 cups sugar
ISAIAH *10:14*	6 eggs
GENESIS *24:17*	1 cup water
EXODUS *3:8*	3 tablespoons honey
I. SAMUEL *30:12*	2 cups raisins
Ibid.	2 cups chopped figs
GENESIS *43:11*	1 cup chopped walnuts

Sift and blend flour, baking powder, salt, and spices. Cream butter and sugar; stir until fluffy. Stir in eggs. Sift about ¼ cup of flour mixture over mixture in bowl and mix well. Stir in about ⅓ cup of water; add remainder of flour and water alternately, stirring between each addition until smooth. Follow Solomon's advice for making good men out of growing boys (PROVERBS *23:13*) and beat well, by hand, at least 8–10 minutes. Add honey, raisins, chopped figs, and walnuts. Stir until well mixed. Pour into 10-inch greased tube pan, and bake at 350°F. for about 90 minutes, until toothpick inserted near center comes out clean.

SALT PORK CAKE

(10–12 servings)

1 cup finely chopped fat salt pork
1 cup boiling water
1 cup molasses
½ teaspoon baking soda
1 cup sugar
1 cup raisins

1 teaspoon cinnamon
½ teaspoon nutmeg
½ teaspoon cloves
½ teaspoon allspice
3 cups flour

Pour boiling water over chopped fat salt pork. Let stand until cool. Dissolve baking soda in molasses. Add to water and salt pork. Add sugar, raisins, and spices. Add flour gradually, and mix well. Pour into 10-inch greased square baking pan, and bake at 350°F. for 45 minutes.

STACK CAKE

(number of servings varies)

This is one of the most popular of all the old-time Christmas desserts. It is just a many-layered plain cake. Make thin layers and spread with homemade jelly. The more layers you have, the better the cake.

STACK PIE

(number of servings varies)

Bake a sweet potato pie, a coconut pie, a custard pie, a mincemeat pie, and an apple pie. After removing from pie plate, stack each pie on top of each other. Press the stack gently, then cut into thin wedges so that everyone gets a taste of each pie.

TEA CAKES

(approximately 24 small cakes)

3½ cups sifted flour
1 teaspoon baking soda
½ teaspoon salt
½ cup butter
1 cup sugar

2 beaten eggs
1 teaspoon vanilla
½ teaspoon nutmeg
½ cup thick sour cream

Sift together flour, baking soda, and salt. Cream butter and sugar. Add beaten eggs, vanilla, and nutmeg. Alternately add flour mixture and sour cream. Beat until smooth. Roll out on floured board to ¼-inch thickness. Sprinkle lightly with sugar. Place on well-greased baking sheet, and bake at 450°F. about 12 minutes, until golden brown. When cool, using cookie cutter or knife, cut into sections suitable for serving.

BUTTERMILK PIE

(8 servings)

3 eggs
1 cup sugar
1 tablespoon butter
4 tablespoons flour
2 cups buttermilk

1 teaspoon lemon extract
1 lemon rind, grated
1 9-inch unbaked pie shell
6 tablespoons sugar (for
    meringue)

Separate eggs; place whites in bowl and set aside. Combine egg yolks and sugar and beat well. Blend butter and flour together. Combine with egg and sugar mixture. Add buttermilk, lemon extract, and grated lemon rind. Mix well. Pour into unbaked pie shell and bake at 450°F. for 10 minutes. Reduce heat to 350°F. and bake 30 minutes longer. Remove pie from oven.

    Beat egg whites until they are stiff. Add sugar, one tablespoon at a time. Continue beating until meringue is stiff but not dry. Spread on top of pie and bake at 400°F. 4–5 minutes or until delicately browned.

MOLASSES PIE
(8 servings)

½ cup flour
½ teaspoon allspice
½ teaspoon cinnamon
½ teaspoon salt
1 teaspoon baking soda

1 cup sour milk
¾ cup molasses
2 beaten eggs
2 tablespoons melted butter
1 9-inch unbaked pie shell

Sift together all dry ingredients except baking soda. Add baking soda to sour milk and molasses. Combine with dry ingredients. Add beaten eggs and melted butter and blend well. Pour into unbaked pie shell and bake at 375°F. until pie begins to brown. Reduce heat to 275°F. and continue baking until filling is firm and will not stick to edge of knife.

SWEET POTATO PONE
(6 servings)

½ cup sugar
½ cup butter
½ cup milk
2 cups grated uncooked sweet
  potatoes

½ teaspoon salt
1 teaspoon allspice
¼ teaspoon cinnamon
½ teaspoon cloves
½ teaspoon nutmeg

Blend sugar and butter; add milk and grated sweet potatoes. Beat well; blend in salt and spices. Place in shallow buttered pan and bake at 325°F. for one hour.

SWEET POTATO PIE

(8 servings)

1½ cups cooked sweet potatoes
1½ cups cream, or evaporated
   milk
6 tablespoons brown sugar
2 tablespoons white sugar
½ teaspoon salt
1 teaspoon cinnamon

½ teaspoon ginger
½ teaspoon cloves
½ cup Karo blue label syrup
3 slightly beaten eggs
1 9-inch unbaked pie shell, with
   high fluted edge

Mash sweet potatoes until free from lumps. Add all ingredients except eggs and mix well. Add eggs and beat slightly. Pour mixture into unbaked pie shell, and bake at 400°F. for about 35 minutes, or until filling will not stick to edge of knife.

BLACKBERRY COBBLER

(6–8 servings)

3 cups blackberries (canned or
   fresh)
1 cup sugar
1 teaspoon lemon juice
3 tablespoons butter

BATTER:
4 tablespoons sugar
1 cup flour
2 teaspoons baking powder
½ teaspoon salt
1 beaten egg

Mix berries, sugar, and lemon juice and spread over the bottom of a well-greased baking dish. Dot with butter.

To make batter, sift dry ingredients, blend in egg, and place on top of fruit. Bake at 375°F. for 30 minutes. If desired, top with whipped cream.

AMBROSIA

(6–8 servings)

6 seedless oranges
1 fresh coconut
1 cup sugar

6 slices of canned pineapple, cut
   into sections (optional)

Peel oranges, remove membrane, and cut into ¼-inch slices. Place slices in a bowl, and set aside. Punch holes in one end of the coconut, drain milk into bowl, and set aside. Place coconut in moderate oven (350°F.) for about 30 minutes, then allow to cool. Break shell with chisel or hammer and remove meat. Break meat into large pieces, peel off brown rind; then grate, using a coarse grater. Place layer of orange slices in bottom of glass serving bowl. Sprinkle grated coconut over slices, topping with 2–3 teaspoons of sugar. Alternate layers of sliced oranges, grated coconut, and sugar. Pineapple may be added to each layer if desired. Refrigerate until thoroughly chilled. Serve with homemade cake.

If desired, the unused coconut milk may be poured over the ambrosia mixture before chilling. The coconut milk also may be used as an ingredient for a fruit punch.

BEATEN BISCUITS

(Louisiana version)
(16–20 biscuits)

3 cups flour
½ teaspoon baking soda
2 teaspoons sugar

1 teaspoon salt
½ cup shortening
¾ cup milk

Sift and blend together dry ingredients. Cut shortening into dry mixture with fork. Add milk quickly and turn out on well-floured board. Remove handle from rolling pin and use this flat end to beat the dough with an up-and-down churning motion. Fold together and beat until dough looks glazed or shiny. Roll out ¾-inch thick, and cut biscuits with floured cutter. Place on cookie sheet and bake at 300°F. for about 30 minutes.

SWEET POTATO CANDY

(approximately 36 pieces)

2 pounds sweet potatoes
2 teaspoons lemon juice
2 pounds sugar

flavor with pineapple juice, lemon juice, orange juice, vanilla, or cinnamon, according to taste

Wash sweet potatoes. Boil or roast with jackets. Peel and put through colander. Place in pan and add lemon juice and sugar. Cook over a low flame, stirring constantly, until mixture separates easily from pan. Set aside to cool. Add flavoring. Take small portions of mixture, dust in sugar, and roll out into long "sticks." Set aside to dry. Wrap in waxed-paper twists.

MOLASSES CANDY

(also known as molasses taffy)
(10 servings)

2 cups sorghum molasses
2 tablespoons butter

1 teaspoon vanilla

Boil sorghum molasses until it reaches the hard ball stage. Remove molasses from stove; add butter and vanilla; stir only enough to mix. Pour into well-greased platter or shallow pan. Let stand until candy begins to stiffen at edges.

To prepare for the fun of "pulling" taffy, butter hands lightly. Take a lemon-size portion of taffy in hands. Pull out and fold back repeatedly until candy changes to a golden color. When taffy begins to harden, either break into sticks or tie into knots or rings, as desired.

JOHNNYCAKE

(4 servings)

¾ cup all-purpose flour
1 teaspoon baking soda
½ teaspoon salt
2 tablespoons sugar
1¼ cup cornmeal

2 beaten eggs
¼ cup white vinegar
1 cup milk
4 tablespoons melted shortening

Sift together flour, baking soda, salt, and sugar. Add cornmeal. Combine eggs, vinegar, milk, and shortening; add to dry ingredients. Stir until just dampened. Turn into lightly greased pan and bake at 400°F. for 30–35 minutes.

VINEGAR PIE

(6 servings)

2 tablespoons butter
¾ cup sugar
3 tablespoons flour
2 teaspoons cinnamon
½ teaspoon cloves
½ teaspoon allspice

1 egg
2 tablespoons vinegar
1 cup water
1 8-inch pie shell, baked
   15 minutes

Cream butter and sugar; add sifted flour, cinnamon, cloves, and allspice to creamed mixture. Blend in egg, vinegar, and water. Cook in top of double boiler until thickened. Pour into partially baked pie shell. Bake at 400°F. about 30 minutes, or until mixture will not stick to edge of knife.

SPOON BREAD

(4 servings)

1 pint milk

1 cup cornmeal

2 tablespoons butter

4 eggs

1 teaspoon baking powder

Place milk in top of double boiler and heat to scalding. Slowly add cornmeal and whip with beater until smooth. Add butter and cook for 20 minutes. Separate eggs; add beaten yolks and baking powder to mixture. Beat egg whites until they peak; fold in. Pour into well-greased baking dish and bake at 350°F. for 45 minutes.

Serve hot with sausages for Christmas breakfast!

"HOG'S-HEAD" CHEESE
(12–14 servings)

1 pig's head
4 pig's feet
2 pig's ears
2 medium-size onions, whole
1 bunch celery, including leafy
   tops

2 bay leaves
¼ teaspoon cayenne pepper
1 teaspoon black pepper
2 tablespoons salt
1 cup vinegar

Place pig's head, feet, and ears in large, deep pot, and add water to cover. Add all seasonings except vinegar; cover pot and boil over low flame 2–3 hours until meat leaves bone. Mince meat coarsely; arrange in mold or pan. Add vinegar to juice remaining in pot. Pour this liquid over meat in mold; refrigerate until mold has set, or congealed. When cold, slice and serve.

Author Index

Title Index